1•2•3 GAMES

No-Lose Group Games
For Young Children

Warren Publishing House, Inc.
P.O. Box 2250, Everett, WA 98203

A special thanks to Sue Foster for experimenting with all the games and for providing valuable suggestions.

Editor: Elizabeth S. McKinnon
Contributing Editor: Sue Foster
Cover Design: Larry Countryman

ISBN 0-911019-09-X

Library of Congress Catalog Card Number 85-050435
Printed in the United States of America

INTRODUCTION

Childhood should be filled with the freedom of discovery, not clouded by the fear of failure. **1•2•3 GAMES** provides parents and teachers with no-lose game suggestions that allow children to experience success by playing together in a spirit of cooperation rather than of competition.

The games are designed to be played by two or more children, either of the same age or of varying ages. Children can enjoy these games at their own developmental levels, thus gaining confidence and self-esteem.

Discover the difference in attitude when young children play games in which everyone wins. Gone are the cheaters, the bullies, the intimidated, the non-participants.

1•2•3 GAMES was written mainly for use when working with groups of preschool children. However, most of the games can be enjoyed by children from age two to eight. The games are especially useful when working with children of mixed ages or skill levels.

1•2•3 GAMES can be used for group times or for parties. For lack of a better word, the games sometimes suggest the giving of prizes. These do not necessarily mean costly items. Children are pleased with rewards such as colorful paper flowers, paper shapes, stickers, rubber stamp pictures, cardboard clowns, badges, raisins, Cheerio necklaces, jingle-bell bracelets and balloons.

Jean Warren

CONTENTS

GROUP GAMES

MOVEMENT GAMES

MUSIC GAMES

STORY GAMES

TITLE INDEX

SWISH, SWISH, MAKE A WISH

AGES: 2-8.

NUMBER OF PLAYERS: 2-10.

MATERIALS: A small broom.

PREPARATION: None.

GAME:

Have the children sit in a large circle. Choose one child to stand in the middle with the broom. Have all the children chant:

> Swish, swish, make a wish.
> What will you be today?

Let the child in the middle choose something or someone he or she would like to be. For example, the child might say "I wish to be a green frog" or "I wish to be Superman." Then have everyone chant:

> Swish, swish, you got your wish.
> Now where would you like to go?

Let the child name a place he or she would like to go, such as Disneyland or the moon. Then have the child jump on the broom and zoom around the inside of the circle while everyone chants:

> Swish, swish, off you go
> On your broom, watch you zoom!

At the end of the chant, give the broom to another child. Continue playing until everyone has had a turn being in the middle.

FUNNY ANIMALS

AGES: 2-4.

NUMBER OF PLAYERS: 1-6.

MATERIALS: A stuffed animal for each child.

PREPARATION: Place stuffed animals in the middle of the room.

GAME:

Have the children sit in a semicircle in front of the stuffed animals. Let one child at a time walk by the animals as everyone recites this verse:

> One day out walking down the street,
> Some funny animals I did meet.
> One made a sound, just like this —
> (Child makes an animal sound.)
> So I took it home and gave it a kiss.

Let the child choose any animal, take it back to the semicircle and give it a big kiss. Continue playing until each child is holding an animal.

GIGGLE-A-THON

AGES: 3-8.

NUMBER OF PLAYERS: 3-10.

MATERIALS: None.

PREPARATION: None.

GAME:

Have the children stand in a circle. Choose one child to be in the middle. Then have the other children take turns trying to make the person in the middle laugh. Give each child a half a minute. If the child makes the person laugh, let him or her have the next turn in the middle. If the person in the middle does not laugh, let him or her choose another child to stand inside the circle. Continue playing until everyone has had a turn being in the middle.

VARIATION:

Have the child in the middle of the circle turn around slowly while everyone tries at the same time to make him or her laugh. When the child laughs, or when three minutes are up, choose another child to stand in the middle.

HOT OR COLD

AGES: 2-5.

NUMBER OF PLAYERS: 3-10.

MATERIALS: An appropriate holiday or seasonal object (a Halloween skeleton, a plastic Easter egg, a Valentine heart, etc.).

PREPARATION: None.

GAME:

Have the children sit with you in a circle. Show them the holiday object and explain that you will be hiding it. Choose one child to be the Searcher. Have the child close his or her eyes while you hide the object. As the child walks around the room searching for the object, let the other children help by calling out "Hot!" if he or she is going in the right direction or "Cold!" if he or she is going in the wrong direction. When the object has been found, let another child have a turn being the Searcher.

PICTURES, PLEASE

AGES: 2-5.

NUMBER OF PLAYERS: 3-10.

MATERIALS: A Polaroid camera, film, paper bag, felt-tip marker.

PREPARATION: Take a Polaroid picture of each child and write the child's name on the back. Put pictures in the paper bag.

GAME:

Have the children sit in a circle. Let one child reach into the bag and pull out a picture. Read aloud the name on the back. Have the child take the picture and go stand in front of the person named. Then help the child recite the following get-acquainted poem:

> Hi, (name of child in picture).
> How do you do?
> (Children shake hands.)
> My name is (name of child holding picture).
> Here's a picture for you.

Have the child give the picture to its owner and then sit down. Continue playing the game, letting the children take turns, until all the pictures have been handed out.

DOODLES

AGES: 2½-8.

NUMBER OF PLAYERS: 2-10.

MATERIALS: A clipboard, paper, crayon or felt-tip marker.

PREPARATION: Attach paper to clipboard.

GAME:

Have the children sit in a circle with you. Tell them they will be working together to make a Doodle Creature, an imaginary animal that no one has ever seen before. Pass the clipboard, along with a crayon or felt-tip marker, around the circle. Let each child draw a line, a circle or any kind of shape on the paper to create a group picture. Keep passing the clipboard around until everyone has had three or four turns. When the children have finished, encourage them to try naming their Doodle Creature.

VARIATION:

Let the children create Doodle Designs.

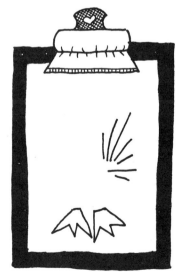  

FOOD FOR THOUGHT

AGES: 4-8.

NUMBER OF PLAYERS: 4-10.

MATERIALS: A food magazine.

PREPARATION: None.

GAME:

Have the children sit with you in a circle while you hold the food magazine. Let one child name a color, come over to you and look through the magazine until he or she finds a food that color. Have the other children try to guess what food has been chosen. Then let the child who guesses correctly either have the next turn or choose another child who has not already had a turn.

VARIATION:

For older children, try using food categories. For example, if a child says "dessert," let him or her find a dessert picture in the magazine. Then have the other children try to guess what dessert the child has chosen.

SHOPPING SPREE

AGES: 2-5.

NUMBER OF PLAYERS: 2-10.

MATERIALS: A table, large paper sack, various objects to use for shopping (food items, toys, household utensils, etc.).

PREPARATION: Place objects on the table.

GAME:

Have the children sit in a circle with you. Give one child the paper sack and send him or her on a "shopping spree." Cover your eyes while the child walks over to the table and chooses an object to put in the sack. Let the other children watch so they know what object has been chosen. When the child returns the paper sack to you, have everyone recite:

> I've been shopping,
> Now I'm back.
> Can you guess
> What's in my sack?

Go around the circle and ask each child a question about the object. For example: "Is it bigger than an apple? Does it have parts that move? Can I eat it? Is it hard or soft?" Let each child have a chance to answer a question. Then try to guess what the object is. When you have named it, have the child return the object to the table. Then choose another child to go off on a shopping spree.

HINT:

If the game is to be played at a party, purchase assorted party favors or inexpensive toys to use as the objects for the shopping spree. Then let the children keep the items they choose to put in the sack as prizes.

TELEPHONE TRIVIA

AGES: 2-8.

NUMBER OF PLAYERS: 3-10.

MATERIALS: A toy telephone, bell, small prizes.

PREPARATION: None.

GAME:

Have the children sit in a circle. Let them pass the toy telephone around the circle until you ring the bell. Have the child holding the phone pick up the receiver and say "Hello, this is (child's name)." Ask the child a trivia question such as "What color is Rudolph's nose?" or "What animal is green, hops and says 'ribbitt'?" Keep giving clues until the child answers correctly. Then let him or her choose a prize. Make sure that each child gets a phone call and that he or she can answer the question you ask.

VARIATION:

For older children, try using a "quiz show" approach. For example: "And now for the $100 bonus question! What frightened away Little Miss Muffet?" Award play money for prizes.

DETECTIVE

AGES: 2-8.

NUMBER OF PLAYERS: 2-10.

MATERIALS: None.

PREPARATION: None.

GAME:

Have the children sit in a semicircle. Choose one child to be the Detective. Describe an object or a person in the room by giving clues such as these: "I'm thinking of something that is red. It bounces. What is it?" Or "Someone in this room is wearing green. Her name begins with an 'M.' She has a big brother named Scott. Who is she?" Then let the Detective move around the room and try to discover the object or person you described. Continue giving clues until the Detective finds what he or she is searching for. Then choose another child to be the Detective.

HINT:

For an authentic touch, give the Detective a large magnifying glass to look through as he or she searches for clues.

COLOR MATCH-UPS

AGES: 2-8.

NUMBER OF PLAYERS: 3-10.

MATERIALS: A different colored piece of construction paper for each child (supplement with different patterned rectangles of wallpaper or giftwrap, if necessary), scissors, paper sack.

PREPARATION: Cut a corner off of each piece of construction paper and put the corners in the paper sack. Place the papers on the snack table to use as placemats.

GAME:

Let the children take turns drawing one of the paper corners from the sack. Then have each child match his or her corner with the corresponding placemat on the table and sit down for snacks. The older children will find their match-ups first, making it easier for the younger children to find theirs.

HINT:

You can also use this approach for handing out party favors. Put pieces of colored paper that correspond to the colors of the party favors in a sack. Then let the children take turns drawing out the pieces. If you're using balloons as favors, give the child who draws out a red piece of paper a red balloon, the child who draws out a yellow piece of paper a yellow balloon, etc.

VARIATION:

For older children, use the same color of paper for all the placemats and cut a puzzle piece out of the corner of each mat. Then have the children match the puzzle pieces with the corresponding placemats.

BUILDING BLOCKS

AGES: 2-8.

NUMBER OF PLAYERS: 2-10.

MATERIALS: Five to ten small building blocks for each child.

PREPARATION: Give each child an equal number of blocks.

GAME:

Have the children sit in a circle with their blocks in front of them. Let one child place the first block in the middle of the circle. Then let the other children take turns stacking one block on top of the other to form a tower. Have everyone count as the blocks are added and the tower grows. Continue the game until the tower falls. Then let the next child start a new tower as everyone begins counting again.

VARIATION:

Instead of a tower, let the children try building a group structure, such as a castle or a spaceship. Have them continue playing until all the blocks have been used.

SHOE MIX-UP

AGES: 2-8.

NUMBER OF PLAYERS: 3-10.

MATERIALS: None.

PREPARATION: None.

GAME:

Have the children each take off one shoe and put it in the middle of the room. While the children cover their eyes, hide the shoes around the room in various places. Let the children search for their shoes and then put them back on. The older children will find their shoes first, making it easier for the younger children to find theirs.

HINT:

Put the younger children's shoes in the more obvious locations.

MUSICAL GRAB BAG

AGES: 2-8.

NUMBER OF PLAYERS: 3-10.

MATERIALS: A large paper bag, prizes, wrapping paper, tape, music.

PREPARATION: Wrap prizes and put them in the paper bag. Set up music, if necessary.

GAME:

Have the children sit in a circle. Start the music and let the children begin passing around the bag filled with prizes. When you stop the music, let the child who is holding the bag reach inside and take out a prize. Then have the child leave the circle and watch as the game continues. Keep playing until everyone has taken out a prize. Then let the children open their prizes all together.

PUZZLE PALS

AGES: 1½-5.

NUMBER OF PLAYERS: 2-10.

MATERIALS: Purchased cardboard party decorations (Halloween characters, birthday scenes, Valentines, etc.) or magazine pictures mounted on construction paper, scissors, small prizes.

PREPARATION: Mount magazine pictures on construction paper, if necessary. Make mini-puzzles (one for each pair of children) by cutting each decoration or picture into two pieces. Cut each puzzle so that the pieces fit together differently.

GAME:

Mix up the puzzle pieces and give a piece to each child. Then have the children move around the room and try to find their "puzzle pals" by matching up their puzzle pieces. As each pair of children completes a puzzle, award small prizes. Since the last two children will be holding matching pieces, everyone will end up a winner.

HINT:

If you have an uneven number of children, you or another adult can participate in the game.

VARIATION:

Separate the halves of the puzzles into two piles. Place one pile on a table or on the floor. From the other pile, give each child one of the puzzle halves. Then let the children take turns looking through the first pile to find their matching puzzle pieces. The older children will find their matching pieces first, making it easier for the younger children to find theirs.

FLASHLIGHT

AGES: 3-8.

NUMBER OF PLAYERS: 2-6.

MATERIALS: A flashlight for each child, a room that can be darkened, magazine pictures (foods, animals, objects, etc.), tape.

PREPARATION: Tape pictures on room walls or ceiling. Darken the room.

GAME:

Have the children sit in a semicircle and give each one a flashlight. Describe the pictures taped on the ceiling or walls by using riddles such as these:

I'm red and juicy.	I'm round and orange.
I grow on a tree.	I grow on the ground.
People eat me.	People carve me on Halloween.
Who am I?	Who am I?

Have the children answer each riddle by shining their flashlights on the picture described.

HINT:

If the game is to be played at a party, you might want to purchase small flashlights and award them as prizes at the end of the game.

VARIATIONS:

Tape four different colors of paper on the ceiling or walls. Name an object and have the children shine their flashlights on the paper that is the same color as that object.

Tape pictures of four different kinds of rooms on the ceiling or walls. Name an object and have the children shine their flashlights on the picture of the room where they would find that object. For example, if you say "bed," have the children shine their flashlights on the picture of the bedroom.

Tape nursery rhyme pictures on the ceiling or walls. Read a rhyme and have the children shine their flashlights on the appropriate picture.

MITTEN MIX-UP

AGES: 1-4.

NUMBER OF PLAYERS: 2-10.

MATERIALS: A different colored or patterned pair of mittens for each child, small pies or pie shapes cut from construction paper.

PREPARATION: Cut out pie shapes, if necessary.

GAME:

Have the children sit in a circle and give them each a pair of mittens. Have each child put one mitten on and place the other mitten in the middle of the circle. Mix up the pile of mittens and let the children search through it to find their mittens' mates. When they have done so, have them put their mittens on and sit back down in the circle. As you play the game, let the children help recite the following poem:

There once were some kittens
Who lost their mittens
And they began to cry,
"Boohoo, Boohoo,
Boohoo, Boohoo,
Now we shall have no pie."

All the kittens
Went to find their mittens —
At least they'd give it a try.
"Hurray, Hurray,"
They wanted to say,
"We hope our mittens we spy."

At last all the kittens
Found their mittens
And they began to cry,
"We found our mittens,
We're good little kittens.
Now we can have our pie!"

When all the children have found their mittens, pass out small pies or pie shapes. The older children will find their mittens first, making it easier for the younger children to find theirs.

VARIATION:

Instead of using real mittens, cut mitten shapes out of construction paper, felt scraps or wallpaper samples and give each child a different colored or patterned pair.

CREATE-A-COOKIE

AGES: 2-8.

NUMBER OF PLAYERS: 1-8.

MATERIALS: A large cookie for each child, frosting in assorted colors, materials for decorating (raisins, coconut, cookie sprinkles, etc.), paper plates, popsicle sticks, small containers.

PREPARATION: Give each child a cookie, a popsicle stick and a paper plate containing small spoonfuls of different colored frosting. Place decorating materials in separate containers in the middle of the work area.

GAME:

Have the children use their popsicle sticks to spread frosting on their cookies. Then pass around the raisins, coconut and other materials and let the children decorate their cookies as they wish. When the game is over, everyone will end up a winner with his or her own cookie to eat.

VARIATION:

For a sugarless alternative, use crackers with a soft cream cheese spread. Let the children decorate their crackers with raisins and dried fruit bits.

24

PICNIC SNATCHER

AGES: 3-8.

NUMBER OF PLAYERS: 3-10.

MATERIALS: A tablecloth or blanket, five to eight picnic items (a plastic spoon, a napkin, a mustard container, etc.).

PREPARATION: Spread tablecloth on the floor. Set picnic items out on the tablecloth.

GAME:

Have the children sit around three sides of the tablecloth. Choose one child to be the Bear, who will act as the "picnic snatcher," and send the Bear off to the "woods" (outside the door or behind a piece of furniture). Ask the rest of the children to look at all the picnic items carefully. Then have them close their eyes and pretend to go to sleep. While they are napping, have the Bear tiptoe out of the woods, snatch one item from the tablecloth, then sneak back into the woods again. Ask the children to wake up and try guessing which item the Bear took. Let the child who guesses correctly either be the next Bear or choose another child who has not already had a turn. Repeat the game until everyone has had a chance to play the part of the picnic snatcher.

HINT:

For younger children, set out fewer items on the tablecloth.

EASTER EGG HUNT

AGES: 2-8.

NUMBER OF PLAYERS: 2-10.

MATERIALS: A lunch sack for each child, various colors of construction paper or wallpaper samples, scissors, glue or stapler.

PREPARATION: Cut the lunch sacks in half and use the bottom halves to make baskets. For each basket, cut a handle out of a different colored piece of construction paper or wallpaper and glue or staple it to the sides of the sack. Then cut six small egg shapes for each basket from paper that matches the handle. Hide the eggs in various places around the room.

GAME:

Give the children each a basket and let them go on an Easter Egg Hunt. When they find eggs that match their handles, have them put the eggs in their baskets. Continue the game until all the eggs have been found.

HINT:

Hide the eggs for each child according to age and ability.

VARIATION:

Let the children help make their own baskets. Before attaching the handles, have the children paint their lunch sacks green. Then, if they are able to use scissors, let them cut fringes along the top edges.

SENT IN BY: Judith Hanson, Newton Falls, OH

TO MARKET, TO MARKET

AGES: 3-8.

NUMBER OF PLAYERS: 3-10.

MATERIALS: None.

PREPARATION: None.

GAME:

Recite the following nursery rhyme with your children:

> To market, to market, to buy a fat pig.
> Home again, home again, jiggety-jig.
> To market, to market, to buy a fat hog.
> Home again, home again, jiggety-jog.

Let each child in turn choose an animal to buy at the market. Have the child make up a nonsense word that rhymes with the name of the animal. For example, if the child chooses to buy a cat, his or her nonsense word might be "jat." Then have everyone recite the rhyme using the two words:

> To market, to market, to buy a fat (cat).
> Home again, home again, jiggety-(jat).

If the next child chooses to buy a chicken and gives "plicken" as a nonsense word, continue the rhyme as follows:

> To market, to market, to buy a fat (chicken).
> Home again, home again, jiggety-(plicken).

Keep playing until everyone has had a turn.

BOWLING

AGES: 2-8.

NUMBER OF PLAYERS: 2-10.

MATERIALS: Five objects to use as bowling pins (empty plastic milk bottles, detergent bottles, juice cartons, stand-up toys, etc.), small prizes, ball (about 6 inches in diameter).

PREPARATION: Set up the five objects in a hallway.

GAME:

Have the children line up a few feet away from the "bowling pins." Let each child roll the ball one or two times to try knocking over the objects. Award prizes to everyone. Control the game by allowing younger children to stand closer to the pins.

HINT:

You might want to number the prizes and hand them out according to the number of pins knocked over.

MIRROR, MIRROR

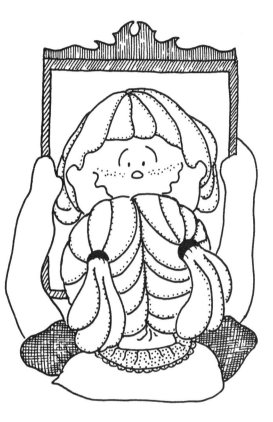

AGES: 2-5.

NUMBER OF PLAYERS: 2-10.

MATERIALS: A small hand mirror for each child.

PREPARATION: None.

GAME:

Have the children sit in a circle and give each one a mirror. Call out a direction such as "Let's make happy faces!" Have everyone recite the rhyme below and then make the appropriate face in his or her mirror:

>Mirror, mirror, who do you see?
>I see a (happy) face looking at me.

Continue the game, each time calling out a direction for making a different kind of face: silly, surprised, grouchy, mean, sleepy, sad, frightened, shy, etc.

HINT:

If the game is to be played at a party, you might want to purchase small plastic mirrors and award them as prizes at the end of the game.

FEED THE ELEPHANT

AGES: 2-8.

NUMBER OF PLAYERS: 3-10.

MATERIALS: A large cardboard box, construction paper, felt-tip marker, scissors, tape, craft knife, peanuts.

PREPARATION: Draw an elephant face on construction paper, cut it out and tape it on the side of the cardboard box. (Or draw a face directly on the side of the box.) Use a craft knife to cut out a hole for the elephant's mouth.

GAME:

Give the children several peanuts each and let them take turns trying to "feed the elephant." Have them line up a few feet away from the box and toss the peanuts into the elephant's mouth. At the end of the game, add more peanuts to the box. Then let each child reach into the box and grab a handful of peanuts. Allow the children to keep and eat all the peanuts they can hold.

LET'S GO FISHING

AGES: 1½-8.

NUMBER OF PLAYERS: 2-10.

MATERIALS: A small fishing pole or a string tied to a stick, magnet, paper clips, construction paper, scissors, tape or glue, prizes, cardboard box.

PREPARATION: Tie the magnet to the fishing line or string. Cut small fish shapes from construction paper and attach a paper clip to each fish. Decorate the sides of the cardboard box with construction paper fish and seaweed shapes. Put the fish in the box.

GAME:

Have the children sit in a semicircle around the cardboard box "ocean." Let them take turns "fishing" for prizes.

HINTS:

You might want to number the fish to correspond with certain prizes. Or use different colored fish to match the colors of the prizes.

If the game is to be played at a party, you might want to have the children fish for small metal friction toys and let them keep the toys as prizes.

VARIATION:

Let the children take turns fishing from a deck or in front of a blanketed-off area. Have them use a small fishing pole with a weight tied to the end of its line. As each child casts out his or her line, have a hidden adult tie a prize onto it.

31

RAINBOW RALLY

AGES: 2-8.

NUMBER OF PLAYERS: 4-12.

MATERIALS: Construction paper (one 9"x12" sheet each of red, orange, yellow, green, blue and purple), scissors, box, gold wrapping paper, tape, small treats for prizes, paper bag.

PREPARATION: Cut a 9-inch square out of each sheet of construction paper. Cut the remaining pieces into 3-inch squares. (You will have one large square and three small squares for each rainbow color.) Place the large squares of paper on the floor, each color in a different area of the room. Place the small squares in the paper bag. Cover the box with gold wrapping paper to make a "pot of gold." Fill the box with treats.

GAME:

Have the children sit in a circle with you. Place the "pot of gold" in the middle. Call out "Rainbow Rally!" and have the children go to any of the areas in the room designated by the colored paper squares. Several children may choose one color area, while some color areas may not be chosen. Reach into the paper bag and pull out one of the small colored paper squares. Then let the children who chose that color area of the room each take a prize from the pot of gold. For example, if you pulled a red paper square from the bag, the children standing near the large red paper square would be the winners. Repeat the process until all the children have won prizes. The odds are that everyone should win two or three times before the game is over.

HINT:

You may want to limit how many times a player can win. For example, you could have players sit back down in the circle after winning two prizes.

TOY CATALOG

AGES: 2-8.

NUMBER OF PLAYERS: 2-10.

MATERIALS: A Christmas toy catalog.

PREPARATION: None.

GAME:

Have the children sit with you in a circle. Show them the toy catalog and discuss which toys they might like to have for Christmas. Let each child take a turn calling out a number between 1 and 10. Turn that number of pages in the catalog as everyone counts together. The child "gets" for Christmas what is pictured on that page.

HINT:

Let older children call out any numbers they wish.

VARIATION:

To add humor to the game, try using an ordinary store catalog. (The children will be in hysterics if you happen to turn to the underwear section!)

TO TELL THE TRUTH

AGES: 4-8.

NUMBER OF PLAYERS: 2-10.

MATERIALS: Magazine pictures (animals, children, toys, food, etc.), construction paper, tape or glue.

PREPARATION: Fold sheets of construction paper in half to make folders. Glue or tape one magazine picture inside each folder.

GAME:

Have the children sit in a circle and give them each a folder containing a picture. Explain that they are to keep their pictures secret. Choose one child to tell something about his or her picture that is either true or false. For example, a child might say "My picture is of a lion sleeping in a jungle." Let the other children show by a raise of hands whether or not they think the child is telling the truth. Then have the child reveal his or her picture to the others. Continue playing the game until each child has had a chance to "tell the truth."

VARIATION:

You can also use the pictures for a guessing game. As one child looks at his or her picture, let the others try to guess what it is. For clues, have the children ask questions such as these: "Is it an animal? Does it have wheels? Is it something to eat?" You may need to help with the questions if the children get stumped.

SNACK ROLL

AGES: 2-8.

NUMBER OF PLAYERS: 3-10.

MATERIALS: A lunch sack, small treats (Cheerios, raisins, pretzels, etc.), one die, chair.

PREPARATION: Fill the lunch sack with treats.

GAME:

Have the children sit in a semicircle facing the chair. Choose one child to be the Mother or Father. Have the child sit in the chair holding the sack and the die. Then let the other children take turns standing in front of the child and saying:

(Mother, Mother/Father, Father), I'm so weak.
May I have a snack to eat?

Have the Mother or Father hand the die to the child. After the child rolls the die, have the Mother or Father give the child the same number of treats as the number that came up on the die. Keep playing the game until every child has had a turn. If you want to continue, let the child who got the most treats be the next Mother or Father.

35

MUSICAL HATS

AGES: 2-8.

NUMBER OF PLAYERS: 4-10.

MATERIALS: A holiday or seasonal hat (a witch hat for Halloween, a Santa hat for Christmas, a snowman hat for Winter, etc.), seasonal music.

PREPARATION: Set up music, if necessary.

GAME:
Have the children sit in a circle. Choose one child to be the Witch, Santa, etc. and give the child the appropriate hat. Have the child sit in the middle of the circle, close his or her eyes, then toss out the hat. Have the child closest to the hat pick it up and start passing it around the circle as you play the music. When you stop the music, let the child holding the hat trade places with the child in the middle and become the new Witch, Santa, etc. Continue playing the game until everyone has had a turn being in the middle.

VARIATIONS:
Let each child try on the hat before passing it on to the next person.

Make the game more general by using three or four different kinds of hats (a firefighter hat, a baseball hat, a stocking cap, etc.). Let the child in the middle of the circle choose which hat he or she wishes to toss out.

FUNNY FACES

AGES: 2-5.

NUMBER OF PLAYERS: 3-10.

MATERIALS: None.

PREPARATION: None.

GAME:

Have the children stand in a line. Ask the first child to turn around to the person behind and make a face. Then have that person try to imitate the face and pass it on to the next child. Let the last child go to the head of the line and make a new face to start the game over again.

VARIATION:

Have the children recite the following rhyme as they make their funny faces:

> Here is my face —
> I give it to you.
> Pass it along —
> Now you're funny, too!

TOM-TOM DANCE

AGES: 2-8.

NUMBER OF PLAYERS: 3-10.

MATERIALS: A tom-tom or an oatmeal box or a coffee can with a plastic lid.

PREPARATION: None.

GAME:

Have the children sit in a circle with their arms crossed. Choose one child to stand in the middle and be the Chief. While the Chief does an Indian dance inside the circle, play the tom-tom with a distinctive beat, such as:

Loud, soft, soft, soft,
Loud, soft, soft, soft.

Vary the tempo of the drumbeat, allowing the Chief to dance slower, then faster. When you stop playing, have the Chief sit down cross-legged in front of another child. Then let that child be the new Chief. Continue playing until everyone has had a turn dancing in the middle of the circle.

HINT:

To set the mood, let the Chief wear a simple Indian headband. Or attach jingle bells to a piece of elastic for the Chief to wear around his or her ankle.

DICE ACTION

AGES: 2½-5.

NUMBER OF PLAYERS: 2-10.

MATERIALS: A color die or a plastic photo cube with squares of different colored construction paper inserted.

PREPARATION: Prepare a color die, if necessary.

GAME:

Have the children sit in a circle. Let one child roll the die and name the color that comes up. Next, have the child call out an action such as "Turn around in a circle!" or "Make a funny face!" Then have everyone who is wearing the color named do the action. For example, if the color blue comes up on the die, the child might say "Everyone wearing blue hop on one foot!" Let the children take turns rolling the die and calling out new actions.

VARIATION:

Cut out pictures of animals and insert them in a photo cube to make an animal die. Let one child roll the die and have the other children pretend to be the animal that comes up.

STUFF THE PILLOW

AGES: 2-8.

NUMBER OF PLAYERS: 3-6.

MATERIALS: A large plastic trash bag, newspapers, scissors.

PREPARATION: Cut the newspapers into large squares.

GAME:

Have the children sit in a circle and give them each a pile of newspaper squares. Place the trash bag in the middle of the circle. Have the children wad up the newspaper squares and stuff them into the trash bag. When the bag is stuffed full, let the children take turns jumping on their large "pillow."

ANIMAL SAFARI

AGES: 2-8.

NUMBER OF PLAYERS: 2-10.

MATERIALS: Various objects for an obstacle course (a two-by-four or a piece of string for a tightrope, a blanket draped over a table for a tunnel, paper circle stepping stones for crossing a river, chairs grouped together for a bridge, scattered pillows for alligators, etc.), animal crackers, bowls.

PREPARATION: Set up an obstacle course, either indoors or outdoors. Put animal crackers in bowls and place one bowl at the end of each obstacle.

GAME:

Let the children take turns "stalking wild animals" by going through the obstacle course. As each child passes through an obstacle, let him or her reach into the bowl at the end and grab a "wild animal" cracker.

HINT:

Use the age and ability of the children to help you decide on the number of obstacles you set up and the number of times the children are to go through the course.

DISAPPEARING DUCKS

AGES: 2-5.

NUMBER OF PLAYERS: 5-10.

MATERIALS: A partition or room divider (a row of chairs or easels, a long piece of furniture, etc.).

PREPARATION: Set up partition, if necessary.

GAME:

Have the children pretend to be little ducks and line up behind you. Lead them around the room and have everyone recite the poem below. Begin the poem with the number of children playing. For six players, start the poem as follows:

> (Six) little ducks went out to play
> Over the hill and far away.
> Mother Duck said, "Quack, Quack, Quack," (softly)
> And (five) little ducks came waddling back.

As you waddle around the room, go behind the partition. Have the child at the end of the line crouch down behind the partition while the other children continue to follow you. Keep repeating the poem, each time leaving a child behind. When all the children are behind the partition, change the last line of the poem to read: "And no little ducks came waddling back." Then recite the last verse of the poem below and have all the children come waddling back out again.

> No little ducks came out to play
> Over the hill and far away.
> Mother Duck said, "Quack, Quack, Quack!" (very loud)
> And (six) little ducks came waddling back.

TEDDY BEAR PARADE

AGES: 2-8.

NUMBER OF PLAYERS: 2-8.

MATERIALS: A Teddy Bear or stuffed animal for each child (ask children to bring favorites from home), a cardboard box for each child, heavy string or rope, materials for decorating (crepe paper streamers, stickers, balloons, precut paper shapes, pompoms, etc.), tape or glue.

PREPARATION: Place decorating materials in the center of the work area.

GAME:

Give the children each a cardboard box and let them use the decorating materials to create "floats" for their Teddy Bears. Attach heavy string or rope to the front of each float to make a handle. Then let the children put their Teddy Bears inside their floats and pull them around the room in a Teddy Bear Parade.

HINT:

Let older children or an adult help the younger children with decorating.

VARIATION:

If weather permits, try an outdoor version of this game. Ask each child to bring from home some kind of riding toy, such as a wagon, bike or scooter. Let the children use crepe paper streamers, balloons, etc. to decorate their vehicles. Then have everyone ride in a parade around the block.

MARIONETTES

AGES: 2-8.

NUMBER OF PLAYERS: 1-10.

MATERIALS: A marionette or a picture of one.

PREPARATION: None.

GAME:

Have the children sit in a circle. Show them a marionette or a picture of one and explain how the puppet moves when someone pulls its strings. Choose one child to stand in the middle of the circle and be the Marionette as you pretend to "pull its strings." Vary the movements by lowering the strings (puppet lies down), bouncing the strings up and down (puppet jumps or dances) and by pretending to pull more than one string at a time (puppet moves one arm and one leg). Continue playing until each child has had a turn.

VARIATION:

You might also try this as a group activity. Let all the children be Marionettes while you pretend to pull everyone's strings at the same time.

COPYCAT

AGES: 2-8.

NUMBER OF PLAYERS: 2-20.

MATERIALS: None.

PREPARATION: None.

GAME:

Have the children stand in a circle and choose one child to be the Leader. Let the Leader show the group a new, crazy way to stand. For example, the child might wrap one leg around the other, bend over and then put both hands on top of his or her head. After demonstrating, have the child call out "Copycat!" Then have the rest of the children do their best to make themselves look exactly like the Leader. Continue playing until each child has had a turn leading the game.

SENT IN BY: Betty Silkunas, Philadelphia, PA

WITCH'S SPELL

AGES: 2-8.

NUMBER OF PLAYERS: 4-20.

MATERIALS: None.

PREPARATION: None.

GAME:

Have the children form a circle and choose one child to be the Witch. Have the Witch stand in the middle of the circle, spin around, then raise his or her hand and cast a magic spell on the rest of the children, turning them all into a particular animal. As the Witch spins, have him or her say:

> Hocus-Pocus, Ala Kazam!
> Turn into (dogs/pigs/etc.) if you can!

Then have the "bewitched" children move around the room pretending to be that animal. After a time, have the Witch spin around again and call out the magic words that will change all the animals back into children:

> Hocus-Pocus, Ala Kazoo!
> Now turn back into you!

Let the children take turns being the Witch.

HINT:

Depending on the age of the children, an adult may need to play the part of the Witch.

TAKE A HIKE

AGES: 3-8.

NUMBER OF PLAYERS: 2-10.

MATERIALS: An index card for each child, felt-tip marker.

PREPARATION: Use the felt-tip marker to draw a different kind of line on each index card. Here are some examples:

GAME:

Have the children sit in a row along one side of the room. Shuffle the index cards and pass them out face down. When you say "Take a hike!" have the children turn their cards over and walk across the room in the manner suggested by the lines on the cards. (If a child makes a mistake, no one will notice because each card is different.) When the children have completed their "hikes," collect the cards, reshuffle them and pass them out again. Keep playing until each child has had the chance to try out several cards.

VARIATION:

For an added challenge, let the children try hopping on one foot, crawling or walking backward as they hike across the room.

47

BUNNY HOP-ALONG

AGES: 2-5.

NUMBER OF PLAYERS: 3-8.

MATERIALS: A large die.

PREPARATION: None.

GAME:

Let one child begin by rolling the die and calling out the number that comes up. (For very young children, have an adult call the numbers.) Then have the child hop that number of times while the other children try to imitate him or her. Let the child try hopping in various ways: forward, backward, to the side or around and around. Encourage big hops and little hops. Continue the game until everyone has had a turn being the leader.

HINT:

Make the game more fun by letting the leader wear a pair of bunny ears fashioned from construction paper. Cut out a 2-inch-wide band, long enough to fit around the child's head. Staple the ends of the band together and attach two paper ears to the back.

SENT IN BY: Judith Hanson, Newton Falls, OH

TIGHTROPE ACT

AGES: 2-5.

NUMBER OF PLAYERS: 2-10.

MATERIALS: Masking tape.

PREPARATION: Place a line of masking tape on the floor to represent a tightrope.

GAME:

Ask the children if they have ever seen a tightrope performer at the circus. Let them take turns sharing their experiences. Then have them line up at one end of the masking tape and take turns using different parts of their bodies to "walk the tightrope." Call out directions such as these: "Walk the tightrope on your toes! Walk the tightrope on your knees! Walk the tightrope using your elbows! Walk the tightrope using your nose!" Regulate the game by giving simpler directions for the younger children and more challenging directions for the older ones.

HINT:

For a fun touch, let the children try carrying a small umbrella as they walk the tightrope.

HERE COMES JACK FROST

AGES: 2½-8.

NUMBER OF PLAYERS: 2-20.

MATERIALS: None.

PREPARATION: None.

GAME:

Have the children sit in a circle. Ask them to name some of their favorite things to do in winter. Then choose one child to be Jack Frost and have him or her wait in a corner of the room or just outside the door. Ask the children to pretend they are each doing one of the winter activities mentioned. As they are "rolling up snowballs" or "skiing down a hill," have Jack Frost come back and move among the children, trying to touch them as he or she goes. Whenever Jack Frost touches someone, have that child "freeze" and stay in the same position without moving. Let the last child to be "frozen" either become the new Jack Frost or choose someone who has not already had a turn. Then have the children act out different activities and repeat the game.

HINT:

Make an "icy crown" for Jack Frost by cutting out the inside of a paper plate and decorating the rim with white crepe paper streamers.

TEDDY BEAR OLYMPICS

AGES: 2-4.

NUMBER OF PLAYERS: 2-10.

MATERIALS: A Teddy Bear or stuffed animal for each child (ask children to bring favorites from home), masking tape, construction paper, scissors, felt-tip marker, ribbon or gold stickers (optional).

PREPARATION: Make awards (one for each Teddy Bear) by cutting small circles out of construction paper and numbering them to indicate First Place, Second Place, etc. Decorate the awards with ribbons or gold stickers, if desired. Make a starting line and a finish line on the floor with masking tape.

GAME:

Have the Teddy Bears line up at the starting line — with their owners, of course! Explain to the children that when you say "Go!" the Teddy Bears are to run as fast as they can to the finish line. (Demonstrate the activity for younger children.) At the end of the race, give out awards to the Teddy Bears, not to the children. In this way, the children will have a chance to participate in a race while avoiding direct competition.

VARIATION:

Let the Teddy Bears and their owners try jumping or crawling as they race to the finish line. Demonstrate each activity first.

WIGGLE WORM

AGES: 2-4.

NUMBER OF PLAYERS: 1-5.

MATERIALS: None.

PREPARATION: None.

GAME:

Have the children sit in a circle. Choose one child to sit in the middle of the circle and be the Wiggle Worm. As everyone recites the poem below, have the Wiggle Worm act out the movements described in the poem.

> One day while I was playing,
> I met a tiny worm.
> Instead of going straight,
> He squirmed and squirmed and squirmed.
>
> Here, now, let me show you
> How he got around.
> He wiggled, wiggled, wiggled
> All across the ground.

Continue playing until every child has had a turn being the Wiggle Worm.

VARIATION:

Fill a small box with sand (or with salt or cornmeal). As you recite the poem, let the children take turns using a finger or a small stick to trace the worm's path in the sand.

MARCHING BAND

AGES: 2-8.

NUMBER OF PLAYERS: 3-10.

MATERIALS: A chair for each child, a rhythm instrument for each child, marching music.

PREPARATION: Arrange chairs in a circle facing out. Place a rhythm instrument on each chair. Set up music, if necessary.

GAME:

Have the children form a circle around the chairs. Play marching music while they march around the circle. When you stop the music, have each child stand in front of the chair closest to him or her and pick up a rhythm instrument. Start the music and let the children play their instruments as they march around. When you stop the music, have them place their instruments back on the chairs. Start the music again and let them begin marching without instruments. Then stop the music and have them each pick up a different instrument to try. Keep playing the game until the children have each had the chance to try several different instruments.

HINTS:

For simple rhythm instruments, try these suggestions:

Sandpaper Blocks: Cover two small wood blocks with sandpaper. Rub together to make sounds.

Drum: Use an oatmeal box or a coffee can with a plastic lid. Beat with hands.

Maraca: Put dried beans or rice in a paper cup. Place another paper cup upside down on top of it and tape the rims together. Shake to make sounds.

BOUNCING BALLS

AGES: 2-8.

NUMBER OF PLAYERS: 1-10.

MATERIALS: None.

PREPARATION: None.

GAME:

Have the children stand around you in a circle. Ask them to pretend they are each holding a small ball. Call out a direction such as "Bounce the ball with your toe!" or "Bounce the ball with your knee!" After a time, call out another direction, such as "Bounce the ball on the ceiling!" or "Bounce the ball on top of your head!" Continue playing as long as interest lasts.

HINT:

Let older children take turns standing in the middle of the circle and giving directions for bouncing the balls.

VARIATION:

To add humor to the game, try having the children pretend to swallow the balls and bounce them inside their bodies.

PARTNER SWITCH

AGES: 2-8.

NUMBER OF PLAYERS: 4-10.

MATERIALS: Music suitable for movement activities.

PREPARATION: Set up music, if necessary.

GAME:
Help each child find a partner. Play the music and have the children perform an action, such as hopping, dancing or skipping, with their partners. You might want to call out the actions: "Partners march!" or "Partners jump!" Or let the children choose their own actions. Each time you stop the music, have the children find new partners.

HINT:
If you have an uneven number of children, choose one child to stand by you and call out an action each time partners are switched.

MUSICAL MATS

AGES: 2-6.

NUMBER OF PLAYERS: 4-8.

MATERIALS: A carpet mat for each child, music.

PREPARATION: Place the carpet mats in a circle. Set up music, if necessary.

GAME:

Have the children sit on the carpet mats, one child to a mat. Start the music and have the children walk around the circle. Take away one mat. When you stop the music, have each child find a mat to sit on or touch in some way (with a foot, hand, elbow, knee, etc.). In order to do this, at least two children will have to share a mat. Continue to start and stop the music, removing one mat each time. As the game progresses, the children will be sharing fewer and fewer mats. When you have one mat left and all the children are sharing it, usually in a heap of giggles, the game is over.

SENT IN BY: Gayle Bittinger, Everett, WA

MAGIC CARPET

AGES: 2-5.

NUMBER OF PLAYERS: 3-12.

MATERIALS: A throw rug or carpet square, marching music.

PREPARATION: Place rug or carpet square in the middle of the room. Set up music, if necessary.

GAME:

Have the children form a line and choose one child to be the Leader. Start the music and let the children march around the room, crossing over the "magic carpet" as they march. When you stop the music, let the child standing on the carpet be the new Leader. Control the game so that each child has a turn leading the line.

SENT IN BY: Betty Silkunas, Philadelphia, PA

GUESS WHO IN THE ZOO

AGES: 2-5.

NUMBER OF PLAYERS: 2-10.

MATERIALS: None.

PREPARATION: None.

GAME:

Have the children sit in a circle to make a "zoo." Ask them to tell about their experiences at the zoo and to name some of their favorite animals. Let each child have a turn going into the zoo and acting out the movements of a different animal. Have the other children try to guess the animal's name. Let the child who guesses correctly either have the next turn or choose someone else to go into the zoo. If the children are unable to guess correctly after three tries, let the actor reveal his or her animal and choose another child to have the next turn.

VARIATION:

Play the same game using farm animals or favorite pets.

THE LIMBO

AGES: 2-8.

NUMBER OF PLAYERS: 4-20.

MATERIALS: A broomstick, music.

PREPARATION: Set up music, if necessary.

GAME:

Have two children hold opposite ends of the broomstick at chest height. Then start the music and let the rest of the children take turns wiggling under the broomstick, trying not to touch it. Ask the two children holding the broomstick to lower it at regular intervals until it is only a few inches from the floor. Then choose two other children to hold the broomstick and do the Limbo again.

HINT:

Try lining up the children from youngest to oldest. This will allow greater success for the younger children and provide more of a challenge for those who are older.

SENT IN BY: Betty Silkunas, Philadelphia, PA

LITTLE RED TRAIN

AGES: 2-6.

NUMBER OF PLAYERS: 2-10.

MATERIALS: None.

PREPARATION: None.

GAME:

Have the children sit down and wait in line at an imaginary train station. Chug around the room as everyone recites the poem below. Each time you stop at the station, have the child at the head of the line hook onto the back of your train. Continue until everyone is hooked on and has had a turn chugging around the room.

> Little Red Train chugging down the track,
> First it goes down, then it comes back.
> Hooking on cars as it goes,
> Little Red Train just grows and grows.

VARIATION:

Let each child choose to be a specific type of car, such as a boxcar or a circus car. Change the third line of the poem to match the type of car chosen. For example, if a child chooses to be a tank car, change the line to read: "Hooking on a tank car as it goes." Let the last child in line be the caboose.

IN AND OUT THE WINDOWS

AGES: 3-8.

NUMBER OF PLAYERS: 5-10.

MATERIALS: None.

PREPARATION: None.

GAME:

Have the children stand in a circle and join hands to form "windows." Choose one child to stand in the middle. Have the child name a creature that flies, such as a butterfly, bee or flying horse. Then let the child pretend to be that creature as he or she "flies" in and out the windows. Have the children in the circle raise and lower their arms as everyone sings:

Sung to: "In and Out the Window"

Fly in and out the windows,
Fly in and out the windows,
Fly in and out the windows,
Little (butterfly/tiny bee/etc.).

Sing the verse twice while the child passes through the windows. Then choose another child to be the next flying creature. Continue playing until all the children have had turns.

TOUCH AND SPIN

AGES: 2-5.

NUMBER OF PLAYERS: 2-10.

MATERIALS: None.

PREPARATION: None.

GAME:

Have the children sit in a circle. Sing the following song with them and have them perform the actions while singing:

Sung to: "Skip to My Lou"

Touch your finger to your nose,
Touch your finger to your nose,
Touch your finger to your nose.
Now spin around with me.

Touch your foot to your knee,
Touch your foot to your knee,
Touch your foot to your knee.
Now spin around with me.

Additional verses:

Touch your arm to your back.
Touch your elbow to your stomach.
Touch your wrist to your ear.

Try making up more verses by encouraging the children to come up with their own ideas. For the last verse, sing:

Touch your toe to your neighbor's toe,
Touch your toe to your neighbor's toe,
Touch your toe to your neighbor's toe.
Now sit right down with me.

SILLY SONGS

AGES: 2-6.

NUMBER OF PLAYERS: 3-10.

MATERIALS: None.

PREPARATION: None.

GAME:

Have the children sit in a circle. Choose one child to name three "silly" words. Then have everyone use the child's words to sing the song below. For example, if the child's three words are "bubbles," "mud" and "popcorn," have the children sing:

> **Sung to:** "The Farmer in the Dell"
>
> (Bubbles), (mud) and (popcorn),
> (Bubbles), (mud) and (popcorn).
> Heigh-ho the derry-oh,
> (Bubbles), (mud) and (popcorn).

Make up new verses for the song by letting each child have a turn naming three silly words.

ZOO TRAIN

AGES: 2½-5.

NUMBER OF PLAYERS: 3-10.

MATERIALS: None.

PREPARATION: None.

GAME:

Have the children line up in a row to make a "zoo train." Designate one area in the room to be the train station. Let the first child in line be the Engineer. Have the children sing the first verse of this song with you:

Sung to: "Down by the Station"

Down by the station,
Next to the zoo,
On came an animal.
Do you know who?

Let the Engineer tell what animal came aboard the train and what action that animal is performing. For example, he or she might say "A kangaroo came aboard and it is hopping." Then let the children sing the rest of the song with you as the train "hops" around the room:

We picked up a (kangaroo),   (Hopping), (hopping), watch us go,
And what do you know.   (Hopping) fast, then (hopping) slow.
This is the way   (Hopping) down, then (hopping) back.
The train started to go.   Watch us (hop) around the track.

When the train returns to the station, have the Engineer go to the back of the line. Then let the child at the front of the line become the new Engineer and choose the next animal. Continue playing until everyone has had a turn being the Engineer.

HINT:

Before playing the game, review various zoo animals and how they move.

NO-LOSE MUSICAL CHAIRS

AGES: 2-5.

NUMBER OF PLAYERS: 3-10.

MATERIALS: A chair for each child.

PREPARATION: Place chairs in a line or in a circle facing out.

GAME:
Lead the children around the row or circle of chairs while singing this song:

> **Sung to:** "In and Out the Window"
>
> Let's walk around the chairs,
> Let's walk around the chairs,
> Let's walk around the chairs,
> And then let's all sit down.

At the end of the song, have each child sit down in the chair by which he or she is standing. Repeat the game as long as the children are having fun.

HINT:
For a "soft touch," try using pillows instead of chairs.

VARIATION:
Continue playing the game, substituting these words for the word "walk": "skip, hop, gallop, crawl."

SENT IN BY: Betty Silkunas, Philadelphia, PA

THE FARMER BY THE WELL

AGES: 2-5.

NUMBER OF PLAYERS: 3-10.

MATERIALS: A table, small bell.

PREPARATION: Place the bell on the table.

GAME:

Have the children sit together in an imaginary barnyard. Ask them to pretend that the table is a wishing well. Choose one child to be the Farmer. Have the Farmer stand by the well as everyone sings:

Sung to: "The Farmer in the Dell"

Oh, farmer by the well,
Oh, farmer by the well.
Make a wish and ring the bell,
Oh, farmer by the well.

Have the Farmer wish for a kind of farm animal. For example, he or she might say "I wish I had some cows." Let the Farmer ring the bell and have the other children grant his or her wish by pretending to be that animal. After a time, have the Farmer call out "Cows come home with me!" Then have the children line up behind the Farmer and follow him or her around the room while everyone sings:

Oh, (cows) come home with me,
Oh, (cows) come home with me.
Heigh-ho away we go,
Oh, (cows) come home with me.

At the end of the song, have the Farmer lead the cows back to the barnyard. Then choose another child to be the next Farmer and repeat the process. Continue playing until every child has had a turn being the Farmer.

66

BIRTHDAY TRAIN

AGES: 2-5.

NUMBER OF PLAYERS: 3-10.

MATERIALS: An index card for each child, yarn, scissors, stapler or hole punch, felt-tip marker.

PREPARATION: Write the age of each child on a separate index card. Make the cards into necklaces by stapling on loops of yarn or by punching holes in the cards and stringing the yarn through the holes.

GAME:

Have the children sit in a semicircle at an imaginary train station. Pass out "tickets" (age card necklaces) and let the children put them on. Call out a number and have the children who are that age get on the Birthday Train. For example, you might say "Everyone who is two climb aboard the Birthday Train!" Then have all the two-year-olds hook on behind you. Lead them around the room as everyone sings:

Sung to: "The Mulberry Bush"

Hop aboard the Birthday Train,
Birthday Train, Birthday Train.
Hop aboard the Birthday Train
If you are (two) years old.

Riding on the Birthday Train,
Birthday Train, Birthday Train.
Riding on the Birthday Train,
Chugging just for you.

Lead the children back to the station and call out a different age. Have those children climb aboard and repeat the process. Keep playing until everyone has had a ride on the Birthday Train.

HINT:

Try letting the older children take turns being the Engineer.

NOAH'S ARK

AGES: 2-8.

NUMBER OF PLAYERS: 4-10.

MATERIALS: None.

PREPARATION: None.

GAME:

Have the children sit in a circle and join hands. Ask them to pretend they are Noah's Ark and that the waves are rocking them all around. Let the children rock back and forth together while everyone sings:

> **Sung to:** "Row, Row, Row Your Boat"
>
> Waves, waves, back and forth,
> Rock the ark all day.
> We row and row so we can go
> Somewhere far away.

At the end of the song, have the children let go of hands to make the ark stop rocking. Then let each child name a pair of animals that is climbing aboard the ark: two dogs, two cats, two alligators, etc. When everyone has had a turn, "pull up the gangplank," have the children join hands and let the ark take off again. Continue playing as long as interest lasts.

THE BEAR WENT OVER THE MOUNTAIN

AGES: 2-8.

NUMBER OF PLAYERS: 2-6.

MATERIALS: None.

PREPARATION: None.

GAME:

Have the children sit in a circle. Start by having everyone sing the first verse of "The Bear Went Over the Mountain":

> The bear went over the mountain,
> The bear went over the mountain,
> The bear went over the mountain,
> And what do you think he saw?

Choose one child to tell what the bear saw. Then have everyone sing the second verse using the child's words. For example, if the child says "a big monster," have everyone sing:

> He saw (a big monster),
> He saw (a big monster),
> He saw (a big monster),
> And what do you think he did?

Repeat the first verse of the song. Then choose another child to tell what the bear saw. Continue until everyone has had a turn.

69

ROW YOUR BOAT

AGES: 2-8.

NUMBER OF PLAYERS: 2-10.

MATERIALS: None.

PREPARATION: None.

GAME:

Help the children form in pairs and show them how to make "boats" with their partners. Have the partners sit on the floor facing each other with legs apart and feet touching. Next, have them stretch forward and hold hands. Then let them pull back and forth while everyone sings "Row, Row, Row Your Boat." At the end of the song, let the children choose new partners.

VARIATIONS:

Have the children sing: "Rock, Rock, Rock Your Boat" (rocking from side to side); "Tip, Tip, Tip Your Boat" (tipping far over to one side, then to the other); "Sail, Sail, Sail Your Boat" (letting go of hands, raising them high overhead and rocking from side to side).

TEENY TINY TALE

AGES: 2-8.

NUMBER OF PLAYERS: 2-10.

MATERIALS: None.

PREPARATION: None.

GAME:

Have the children sit in a circle. Encourage them to use their "teeny tiny" voices as they help you tell an open-ended story such as the following:

> Once upon a time there was a teeny tiny _____ who
> lived in a teeny tiny _____. (He/She) had a teeny tiny
> _____ which (he/she) kept in (his/her) teeny tiny
> _____. One day, (he/she) went to a teeny tiny
> _____ and got a teeny tiny _____.

Continue the story until each child has had at least one chance to contribute an idea.

HINT:

As a follow-up, the children might enjoy illustrating the story or acting it out.

VARIATION:

Have the children use their "giant" voices to help you tell an open-ended story. Follow the same procedure described above.

DEAL-A-STORY

AGES: 2-8.

NUMBER OF PLAYERS: 2-10.

MATERIALS: A deck of cards.

PREPARATION: None.

GAME:

Have the children sit in a circle. Deal two or three cards face down to each player. Choose one child to turn over a card. Use the number or picture on the card as you begin telling a story. Then continue around the circle, letting each child turn over a card, and incorporate the numbers and pictures into your story. A sample story would be as follows:

(Child turns over a ten.)	Ten little rabbits went to town.
(Next child turns over a four.)	They went to four houses looking for food.
(Next card is a queen.)	At the last house, they met a beautiful lady.
(Next card is a seven.)	She gave them seven carrots.
(Next card is a jack.)	As the rabbits started to leave, a little boy chased them.
(Next card is a two.)	They ran down two paths that led into the woods.
(Next card is a three.)	In the woods, they found three holes which they jumped into safely with all their carrots.

Continue playing until each child has turned over at least one card.

HINT:

Let older children take turns being the storyteller.

FLANNELBOARD FROLICS

AGES: 3-8.

NUMBER OF PLAYERS: 2-10.

MATERIALS: A flannelboard, felt pieces, scissors, box or paper bag.

PREPARATION: Cut out 10 to 12 different felt shapes (a car, a house, a ball, a boat, a cat, a tree, a child, a dinosaur, a flower, etc.). Place the shapes in a box or paper bag.

GAME:

Have the children sit in a semicircle facing the flannelboard. Choose one child to reach into the box or bag and take out one of the felt shapes. When the child places the shape on the flannelboard, start telling a story about the shape. Then let the other children take turns placing shapes on the flannelboard. As they do so, incorporate the shapes into the story. Have the children place the shapes in a line from left to right to form a "storyline." A sample story would be as follows:

(Child places house on board.)	Once there was a small white house.
(Next child places tree on board.)	That small white house just happened to be next to a tall, tall tree.
(Next shape is a cat.)	A furry cat named Penelope slept by the fireplace in the small white house next to the tall, tall tree.
(Next shape is a dinosaur.)	One day, Penelope looked out the window and saw a big green dinosaur.
(Next shape is a ball.)	He was bouncing a ball against the trunk of the tall, tall tree.

Continue the story until each child has had a chance to place at least one shape on the flannelboard.

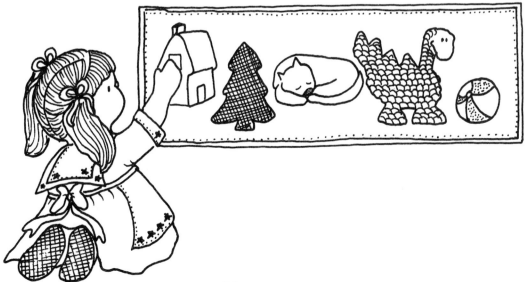

73

VERY HUNGRY CATERPILLARS

AGES: 2-6.

NUMBER OF PLAYERS: 2-6.

MATERIALS: *The Very Hungry Caterpillar* by Eric Carle.

PREPARATION: None.

GAME:

Have the children sit with you in a semicircle while you read aloud *The Very Hungry Caterpillar*. Let your children retell the story, taking turns naming all the things the caterpillar ate. At the end of your version of the story, have the children pretend to be "very *full* caterpillars" who roll up into balls and go to sleep. When you clap your hands and say "Caterpillars wake up!" have them slowly unroll, flap their beautiful new wings and pretend to fly away. Let them "fly" around the room for a few minutes. Then clap your hands and say "Butterflies land!" When the children are seated, let them take turns telling where they would fly away to if they had wings.

CHOOSE YOUR OWN ADVENTURE

AGES: 2-8.

NUMBER OF PLAYERS: 2-10.

MATERIALS: A paper bag, 10 to 12 small objects (a toy car or truck, a plastic animal or person, a spoon, a crayon, a button, etc.).

PREPARATION: Put objects in the paper bag.

GAME:

Have the children sit in a circle with you. Draw an object out of the bag and use it to begin telling a story. Then let each child have a turn drawing an object out of the bag. After the child names the object, weave it into the storyline. For example, if you draw out a plastic dog, you might begin: "Once there was a little brown and white dog named Patches." If a child then draws out a toy firetruck, you might continue: "Whenever there was a fire, Patches got to ride with the firefighters on the firetruck." Continue the story until everyone has had at least one turn drawing an object out of the bag.

HINT:

Older children might enjoy telling their own stories as they draw the objects out of the bag.

THE END !

TITLE INDEX

Activities, songs and new ideas to use right now are waiting for you in every issue of the TOTLINE newsletter.

Each issue puts the fun into teaching with 24 pages of challenging and creative activities for young children, including open-ended art activities, learning games, music, language and science activities.

Sample issue
$1.00

One year subscription (6 issues) $15.00

Beautiful bulletin boards, games and flannelboards are easy with PRESCHOOL PATTERNS.

You won't want to miss a single issue of PRESCHOOL PATTERNS with 3 large sheets of patterns delightfully and simply drawn. Each issue includes patterns for making flannelboard characters, bulletin boards, learning games and more!

Sample issue
$2.00

One year subscription (6 issues) $18.00

Totline Books

Super Snacks - 120 seasonal sugarless snack recipes kids love.

Teaching Tips - 300 helpful hints for working with young children.

Teaching Toys - over 100 toy and game ideas for teaching learning concepts.

Piggyback Songs - 110 original songs, sung to the tunes of childhood favorites.

More Piggyback Songs - 195 more original songs.

Piggyback Songs for Infants and Toddlers - 160 original songs, for infants and toddlers.

Piggyback Songs in Praise of God - 185 original religious songs, sung to familiar tunes.

Piggyback Songs in Praise of Jesus - 240 more original religious songs.

Holiday Piggyback Songs - over 240 original holiday songs.

1•2•3 Art - over 200 open-ended art activities.

1•2•3 Games - 70 no-lose games for ages 2 to 8.

1•2•3 Colors - over 500 Color Day activities for young children.

1•2•3 Puppets - over 50 puppets to make for working with young children.

1•2•3 Murals - over 50 murals to make with children's open-ended art.

1•2•3 Books - over 20 beginning books to make for working with young children.

Teeny-Tiny Folktales - 15 folktales from around the world plus flannelboard patterns.

Short-Short Stories - 18 original stories plus seasonal activities.

Mini-Mini Musicals - 10 simple musicals, sung to familiar tunes.

Small World Celebrations - 16 holidays from around the world to celebrate with young children.

"Cut & Tell" Scissor Stories for Fall - 8 original stories plus patterns.

"Cut & Tell" Scissor Stories for Winter - 8 original stories plus patterns.

"Cut & Tell" Scissor Stories for Spring - 8 original stories plus patterns.

Seasonal Fun - 50 two-sided reproducible parent flyers.

Theme-A-Saurus - the great big book of mini teaching themes.

Available at school supply stores and parent/teacher stores or write for our FREE catalog.

Warren Publishing House, Inc. • P.O. Box 2250, Dept. B • Everett, WA 98203